MY OLD
Kentucky
ROAD TRIP
★

FAMOUS KENTUCKY FLAVORS

EXPLORING THE COMMONWEALTH'S GREATEST CUISINES

CAMERON M. LUDWICK

&

BLAIR THOMAS HESS

Photography by ELLIOTT HESS

INDIANA UNIVERSITY PRESS

This book is a publication of

Indiana University Press
Office of Scholarly Publishing
Herman B Wells Library 350
1320 East 10th Street
Bloomington, Indiana 47405 USA

iupress.indiana.edu

The paper used in this publication meets the minimum
requirements of the American National Standard
for Information Sciences—Permanence of Paper for
Printed Library Materials, ANSI Z39.48-1992.

Manufactured in the United States of America

Cataloging information is available from the Library of Congress.

ISBN 978-0-253-04510-2 (cloth)
ISBN 978-0-253-03925-5 (paperback)
ISBN 978-0-253-03926-2 (ebook)

1 2 3 4 5   24 23 22 21 20 19

All photos by Elliott Hess unless otherwise noted,
www.elliotthess.com.

*To our culinary inspirations
and those who inspired them.
Thank you for your patience and advice—
about cooking and all the rest.
We cherish our times spent together
in full, messy kitchens.*

Contents

Acknowledgments

We consider ourselves experienced roadtrippers and even more seasoned eaters of good food. This left us uniquely poised to become experts of the state's food festival scene and the history of the foods that inspired the celebrations. Or so we thought. As it turns out, there's more to writing a food book than just being willing and able to eat food. Consider it a lesson learned.

We are forever indebted to our fabulous photographer, Elliott Hess (**www.elliotthess.com**), who not only spent hours giving the Glamour Shots treatment to our food but also labored in the kitchen day after day to cook every famous Kentucky culinary creation that we dreamed up. We can't express how thankful we are for our personal goetta- and chicken-fryin', hot brown–stackin', burgoo-simmerin', beer cheese–brewin', pie-bakin' wonder chef. Oh, and he managed to take a few photos too.

Thanks to Ashley Runyon and her team of miracle workers at Indiana University Press, who so gracefully handle our ramblings.

And to our dear friend Alice at Speilburg Literary Agency: thank you for knowing when to push and when to pull. Your patience and wisdom are almost as invaluable as your years of friendship. Almost. As usual, we couldn't have pulled this off without you.

We can't possibly give enough praise to the hardworking Kentuckians across the Commonwealth who volunteer their time to put on these food celebrations each year. From the smallest task to the world-record-sized undertakings, please know that we appreciate all you do to make these unforgettable experiences for all of us.

We often tell folks that while we usually like what we see when we get there, in this line of work, it's more about the journey than the destination. In this case we discovered that it's more about the time spent together in the kitchen—the laughter, the stories, the tears, the fun—than it is about what you pull out of that oven. Even when there are delicious results.

We hope Colonel Sanders and Carl Kaelin and Ruth Hanly had as much fun in the kitchen as we did and that they learned as much from their parents and grandparents as we managed to—about cooking and the tougher stuff, too. Thank you to our families for the years of time spent together in the kitchen and all of the great things that came out of it. It's a tradition we hope to pass on to our littlest and hungriest roadtripper.

And more than anything, thanks to those who do the dishes.

Calendar of Kentucky Food Festivals

Here is a guide to some of our favorite food festivals across the state. Please check the event websites for up-to-date schedules and information. Bon appétit!

APRIL

Tater Day—Benton
Spring Chicken Festival—Clinton
Mountain Mushroom Festival—Irvine

MAY

International Bar-B-Q Festival—Owensboro

JUNE

Seedtime on the Cumberland—Whitesburg
Poke Sallet Festival—Harlan
Beer Cheese Festival—Winchester

JULY

Louisville Blues, Brews & BBQ Festival—Louisville
Bacon, Bourbon, and Brew Festival—Newport
Green River Catfish Festival—Morgantown

AUGUST

Goettafest—Newport/Covington
Great Inland Seafood Festival—Newport
Crave Food and Music Festival—Lexington

SEPTEMBER

Monroe County Watermelon Festival—Tompkinsville
Mainstrasse Oktoberfest—Covington
Pecan Festival—Hickman
Banana Festival—Fulton
Kentucky State BBQ Festival—Danville
Kentucky Bourbon Festival—Bardstown
Spoonbread Festival—Berea
Casey County Apple Festival—Liberty
World Chicken Festival—London
Anderson County Burgoo Festival—Lawrenceburg
Morgan County Sorghum Festival—West Liberty
BBQ on the River—Paducah
Marion County Country Ham Days—Lebanon
Seven Springs Sorghum Festival—Sulphur Well

OCTOBER

Trigg County Country Ham Festival—Cadiz
Kentucky Apple Festival—Paintsville

FAMOUS
KENTUCKY
FLAVORS

Introduction

President Abraham Lincoln once said, "Food is essential to life, therefore make it good." Or perhaps that was one of our grandmothers who said that. Come to think of it, Kentucky's great Honest Abe was probably too busy changing the course of history to comment on good food, but we have no doubt that he was an appreciator of a home-cooked Kentucky meal. We can say this with confidence because food is a place of common ground—it's a universal experience that all creatures on the planet share in. Our friend Abe would appreciate that.

In Kentucky, there is a rich culinary history of meals shared and recipes cooked from a wide variety of backgrounds brought in by the settlers who forged through the Cumberland Gap and established the communities we inhabit today. Our food is as unique and diverse as our people, and from our beer-infused cheese and fried chicken to our spoonbread and candy made with bourbon, we Kentuckians know a thing or two about good eatin'.

Just ask our grandmothers. They'll meet you at the door with a one-armed hug and a "Didge-eat-jet?" (That's "Have you eaten within the hour?" for you nonnatives.) And no matter your collective answers, there's a plate warming in the oven for all y'all.

As kids, we just assumed our grandmothers invented those cheese omelets or bowls of oatmeal with grape jelly piled on top. And while our childhood innocence may have given the grannies more credit than they deserved, the Bluegrass State is, in fact, full of notable chefs and accidental kitchen geniuses who have invented—or at least have secured the bragging rights for inventing—some pretty famous culinary delights.

Ever enjoyed a salad of Bibb lettuce? Well, then you can thank lawyer and amateur horticulturist John B. Bibb of Frankfort, Kentucky, who developed the variety of butterhead lettuce in the 1860s. Sometimes called a "limestone lettuce," when it is grown in alkaline, limestone-derived soils, Kentucky's Bibb lettuce is particularly sweet, which led to its popularity. The heirloom lettuce variety achieved national recognition in the 1920s and was served at upscale restaurants around the country. Bibb lettuce has seen a recent surge in popularity because it grows well in hydroponics and aquaponics systems, which use fish and water but no soil to grow vegetables.

Impressed? We haven't even gotten to the main course.

For you carnivores who'd prefer a cheeseburger, Kentucky is here for you, too. Adding cheese to your beef and bun combo became popular in the 1930s, and here in Kentucky, every good citizen and burger enthusiast knows that the cheeseburger was invented at Kaelin's Restaurant in Louisville. Carl Kaelin and his wife, Margaret, opened their restaurant on Newburg Road in 1934 and shortly after tossed a slice of cheese (the American variety, despite Carl's Swiss ancestry) on a beef patty creating a truly American culinary staple.

While others have certainly claimed the cheeseburger—we're looking at you, Humpty Dumpty Drive-In in Denver, Colorado—Kentuckians trust Irma Kaelin Raque, Carl and Margaret's daughter, who began helping her mother take hamburger (and cheeseburger) orders as a three-year-old. The way Irma tells it, her mother was cooking burgers one day when her father casually suggested putting cheese on them. He promptly finished three of them in one sitting. And while the original restaurant closed in 2009, plans to reopen and serve the iconic cheeseburger are in the works.

We're getting full already, so don't even get us started on our mint juleps. History may tell you that similar drinks were popular in the American colonies, but the cocktail as we know it today was invented—or at least perfected—at the famous Churchill Downs, home of the Kentucky Derby. Meriwether Lewis Clark Jr.

(if that name sounds familiar, it's because he is the grandson of William Clark of the Lewis and Clark expedition fame) built Churchill and inaugurated the very first Kentucky Derby in 1875. Back then, julep cups were often used as prizes for races won, so it only made sense that good Kentuckians would take their bourbon not just with but *in* their trophy.

The delightful concoction of bourbon (also invented in Kentucky, so you can trust that we're good at this particular mixology), sugar, water, shaved ice, and fresh mint is a Kentucky staple year-round, though only at the Derby will you see 127,000 of them consumed in one weekend. If you're indulging, might we suggest using Old Forester, as they do at Churchill Downs, and spearmint. Believe it or not, there is actually a cultivar of spearmint called "Kentucky Colonel." Cross our hearts.

Y'all, we're only just gearing up. Grab a plate and join us on a culinary tour across the Bluegrass State. If you need a snack in between courses, grab a Kentucky-famous Ale-8-One soft drink and a Blue Monday candy bar. You won't regret it.

In true *My Old Kentucky Road Trip* fashion, we welcome all of you to our table to share some of our favorite Kentucky foods and the festivals that celebrate them. The only thing we like more than telling you about all of this great Kentucky cuisine is actually eating it. We think you'll agree.

Part One
STARTERS

1 | Beer Cheese

It is probably traditionally assumed that one should pair cheese with wine, and in Kentucky we are plenty respectful of that palate pleaser—so much so that when it came to partnering cheese with other alcoholic libations, we thought we'd make it real easy and just mix it all together.

Meet beer cheese.

This delightful Kentucky culinary invention is a cheese spread that usually has a sharp cheddar flavor—most varieties start with sharp cheddar cheese. To this base, we add enough beer to provide flavor and texture, and from there, it's up to the artisans. Many use garlic and a variety of spices that might include dry mustard, horseradish, and cayenne pepper. Some are mild, many are hot, and all are absolutely delicious. They are traditionally served with veggie slices and saltine crackers, though we're sure you could dress it up if you choose.

In typical Kentucky fashion, there are conflicting stories about the origins of beer cheese, but by most accounts, the spicy spread was first served in the 1940s by Johnnie Allman at the Driftwood Inn in Winchester. Allman, a native of Richmond, was a former newspaper reporter and police officer before opening his first restaurant on the banks of the Kentucky River, near Boonesborough. There he first served his now-famous Snappy Cheese, a recipe he perfected with his cousin, Joe, who lived in Phoenix, Arizona. Perhaps that southwestern influence explains why most beer cheese is spicy.

Johnnie moved his restaurant to the site where Hall's on the River sits today (where you can get a fantastic beer cheese) and sold the business years later. Allman stayed in the restaurant business until 1978, when his latest brick-and-mortar burned down and was never rebuilt. The last genuine Allman's beer cheese was served at Allman's closed restaurant—until recently, when Johnnie's grandson, Ian, and his wife, Angie, began preparing small batches using the original ingredients and selling the cheese again in select grocery stores as Allman's Beer Cheese.

In 2013, Kentucky truly claimed beer cheese as its own, and the Kentucky Legislature decreed Clark County as its birthplace.

Outside of Kentucky, this dairy delicacy is gaining popularity across the country, though most makers will leave you on your own when you ask for a recipe. It's like asking Grandma for her chocolate pie recipe—they'll give you the basics ("Well, you start with cheese and add some beer"), but they're not likely to tell you the type of beer or the spices that go into their individual batches. Those specifics are held close to the vest, which adds to the enjoyment of trying all the different varieties.

Look for beer cheese with the pimento and Palmetto Cheese spreads in your grocery store or at your favorite party store. While you're in Kentucky, consider taking a trip down the Beer Cheese Trail. Grab your official Beer Cheese Trail Log at any of the eight participating restaurants on the trail, which include Cairn Coffee House, Hall's on the River, Waterfront Grille & Gathering, JK's at Forest Grove, Full Circle Market, Woody's Sports Bar & Grill, Gaunce's Deli & Cafe, and DJ's Bar & Grill. Learn more at **www.beercheesetrail.com**.

Order a beer cheese item from the menu at these restaurants, and collect stamps for your log. When you've visited at least five, return your cheese log to the Winchester Tourism Office for a free T-shirt! For you overachievers who visit all eight stops, you will be entered for a chance to become a Beer Cheese Festival judge. There is no higher honor.

A Classic Kentucky Beer Cheese

2 10-ounce pieces of extra sharp cheddar cheese

2 cloves garlic

1 7-ounce bottle beer (of your choice, but we'll recommend a dark stout, if you have it)

1/8 teaspoon salt

Hot sauce to taste

Grate cheese and garlic in a food processor; adding the remaining ingredients, mix until thoroughly blended. The mixture will be soft but will harden in the refrigerator. Serve with crackers, celery sticks, radish roses, and pretzels.

★ A ROAD TRIP TO THE BEER CHEESE FESTIVAL IN WINCHESTER ★

While you can enjoy the Beer Cheese Trail any time of year, it is only on a special—and always scorching—weekend each June that you can experience the one-of-a-kind Beer Cheese Festival

Visitors to the annual Beer Cheese Festival in Winchester get to sample recipes from various vendors and vote for their people's choice. A juried beer cheese competition also takes place at the event.

in Winchester. Each year, thousands of festival-goers descend on Beer Cheese Boulevard (known as Main Street the other fifty-one weeks out of the year) to taste beer cheese from makers from across the country and cast their votes for the People's Choice Award while they're sampling.

Don't forget to take some home with you. When Queen Elizabeth II, the queen of England, visited Churchill Downs in Louisville in 2007, she was photographed carrying a container of beer cheese as she boarded her plane at Bluegrass Airport. We'll count that as a royal stamp of approval.

★ IF YOU GO

The Beer Cheese Festival is held in downtown Winchester usually around the second weekend in June each year. Check **www.beer cheesefestival.com** for the up-to-date schedule. While you're at the festival, make sure to grab an Ale-8-One in its iconic green glass bottle, another Winchester tradition. This ginger soft drink was invented in Kentucky by G. L. Wainscott in 1926 at his plant

Goetta is a meat and grain sausage inspired by the German cooking of settlers who migrated to northern Kentucky in the eighteenth century. It is made of ground meat, oats, and spices.

on North Main Street in Winchester. Wainscott's great-great nephew still uses the original recipe today. Learn more at **www .ale8one.com**.

★ A ROAD TRIP TO THE MAINSTRASSE VILLAGE GOETTAFEST IN COVINGTON ★

Perhaps one of Kentucky's best-kept secrets is Covington's Mainstrasse, a nineteenth-century German neighborhood that features unique shops and galleries and a variety of great restaurants, beer and bourbon pubs, and options for live music. Throughout the year, the village hosts several fun festivals—you really should make it to this river town for Maifest in May and Oktoberfest in September. But none is so unique as Goettafest, which celebrates a unique sausage product.

For those of you furrowing your brows and trying to pronounce this oddity (Kentuckians say "ged-da" or "get-uh," but our German ancestors probably pronounced it "gutta"), we'll assume you've never tried this culinary delight, and to that we have one thing to say: you gotta get you some goetta.

Mainstrasse in Covington is a nineteenth-century German neighborhood that features unique shops and galleries and a variety of great restaurants, beer and bourbon pubs, and options for live music.

Goetta is a meat and grain sausage inspired by German cooking that is incredibly popular in northern Kentucky and Cincinnati, Ohio. It is made up of ground meat (usually pork or pork and beef), steel-cut oats, onion, and a collection of spices. It was traditionally considered a peasant dish meant to stretch out servings of meat over several meals and came with German settlers when they emigrated to the southern Ohio and northern Kentucky area along the Ohio River in the eighteenth century. Today, northern Kentuckians help their Cincinnati neighbors consume more than one million pounds of goetta annually.

Need help with the cooking part? Just slice your goetta sausage in half-inch patties, much like you'd prepare traditional breakfast sausage, and brown it in a skillet over medium heat.

★ IF YOU GO

The annual MainStrasse Village "Original" Goettafest is held every June in the village. Visit **www.mainstrasse.org/goetta fest** for an up-to-date schedule of events. Glier's, a major producer of goetta in Covington, also hosts a Goettafest in Newport, Kentucky, in August. Learn more at **www.goetta.com**.

2 | Spoonbread

For those of you who think you've had cornbread in all its forms, you haven't lived until you've tasted Kentucky spoonbread. Often described as a cornbread soufflé or a savory pudding (think Yorkshire pudding), spoonbread has a sort of cultlike following of folks who swear by this traditional cornmeal dish, which has been popular for more than a century in Kentucky and further south.

People love spoonbread for the folklore of the dish as much as for its taste, and it pulls at the heartstrings of Kentucky's most southern traditionalists, who are proud to honor those of the state's culinary roots that run far beneath the Mason-Dixon line.

Facing: Spoonbread is often described as a cornbread soufflé or a savory pudding and is perhaps most famous in Kentucky at Boone Tavern in Berea.

It's a mix of cornmeal, butter, eggs, milk, and seasonings, and it is served piping hot by the—yes, you guessed it—spoonful, with butter, honey, or sorghum (a Kentucky favorite) on top. When made properly, it has a fluffy, custardy interior with a crunchy crust.

Tracing the origins of spoonbread is a lot like studying the history of early pioneer Kentuckians. Suppone—or Indian corn—was a popular crop for early settlers in the state, and milling it into cornmeal was one of the Commonwealth's earliest agriculture industries. As families settled in Kentucky, they developed recipes using what was most available to them and what they could make in large quantities to feed growing populations with few resources. Cornbread and spoonbread are products of these early recipes, and most spoonbread ingredients remain the same.

A proud staple of the southern United States, spoonbread is perhaps most famous in the Bluegrass State at Boone Tavern in

Copycat Boone Tavern Spoonbread

3 cups milk	2 tablespoons butter
1¼ cups cornmeal	1¾ teaspoons baking powder
3 eggs	1 teaspoon salt

Stir meal into rapidly boiling milk. Cook until very thick, stirring constantly to prevent scorching. Remove from heat and allow to cool. The mixture will be cold and very stiff. Add well-beaten eggs, salt, baking powder, and melted butter. Beat with electric beater for fifteen minutes. (If hand beating is used, break the hardened cooked meal into the beaten eggs in small amounts until all is well mixed.) Then beat thoroughly for ten minutes using a wooden spoon. Pour into well-greased casserole dish. Bake thirty minutes at 375 degrees F. Serve from the dish by spoonfuls.

Berea hosts the Spoonbread Festival in Berea each September and features arts and crafts, bluegrass music, a car show, and its delicious namesake.

Berea. Richard T. Hougen, longtime manager of Boone Tavern Hotel, started the custom of serving guests a complimentary scoop of spoonbread before they began their meal. He called the bread the richest, lightest, and most delicious of all cornmeal breads, and the tavern still serves one of its most popular recipes today.

If you are in search of unbolted, fresh white cornmeal, visit the historic Weisenberger Mill in Midway. In operation since 1865, this picturesque mill produces a wide variety of delicious mixes.

★ A ROAD TRIP TO THE SPOONBREAD FESTIVAL IN BEREA ★

Each September, one of the most unique towns in Kentucky celebrates one of the most unique culinary creations. The Spoonbread Festival in Berea serves up a hearty helping of this sweet cornbread soufflé with a side of Kentucky hospitality.

Berea, located about forty miles southeast of Lexington, is the artisan capital of the Bluegrass State. Home to an incredible community of working artists and innovative chefs, Berea is a great destination for delicious local food and beautiful works of art.

In late summer, Berea is also home to the heartwarming Spoonbread Festival. From its hot-air balloon glow and car show to its hundreds of artisan booths and lines of food vendors, the festival is the perfect end to the long Kentucky summers. Don't leave without your scoop of spoonbread—the festival's namesake is served hot by a team of wonderful volunteers. Enjoy yours with a side of bluegrass music and good company—it's our absolute favorite way to celebrate the dish.

★ IF YOU GO

The Spoonbread Festival is held in the middle of September each year at Memorial Park in Berea, easily accessible from Interstate 75. Visit **www.spoonbreadfestival.com** for current dates and schedules of events. While you are in town, stop for decadent food (and yes, spoonbread) at the historic Boone Tavern (**www.boonetavernhotel.com/dining**) or enjoy incredible baked goods from locally grown ingredients at Native Bagel Co. (**www.nativebagelcompany.com**). Make sure to visit the Artisan Village for one-of-a-kind art treasures, and circle back to Chestnut Street for eclectic and antique gifts. Discover more at **www.visitberea.com**.

★ A ROAD TRIP TO GEORGETOWN'S SWEET CORN FESTIVAL ★

Sweet corn has been a favorite crop for Kentucky farmers since the state was founded in 1792. The earliest settlers through the Cumberland Gap found that corn grew amazingly well in the future Bluegrass State, and it has remained important to our state's agriculture industry and culture ever since—after all, we have corn to thank for bourbon.

Corn Pudding

5 eggs

⅓ cup melted butter

¼ cup white sugar

½ cup milk

4 tablespoons cornstarch

2 cans whole kernel corn, 1 can drained

2 cans cream-style corn

Preheat oven to 400 degrees. In a large bowl, beat eggs. Add melted butter, sugar, and milk. Whisk in cornstarch, and stir in corn and creamed corn. Blend well. Pour mixture into a two- to three-quart greased casserole dish, and bake for one hour.

So it is no surprise that Kentuckians like to celebrate sweet corn each summer with the Sweet Corn Festival at Evan's Orchard and Cider Mill in Georgetown. Enjoy a day of local crafts, live music, hayrides, and—of course—corn on the cob at one of the best agritourism destinations in Central Kentucky. If you're hungry, whip up a dish of corn pudding. This concoction of stewed corn, eggs, sugar, butter, milk, and cornstarch is a food staple in the southern United States, particularly in the Appalachian regions of Kentucky.

★ IF YOU GO

Sweet Corn Festival and Farm Day takes place in July each year at Evan's Orchard and Cider Mill located off Newtown Pike (KY-922) in Georgetown, about twelve miles north of Lexington. Visit **www.evansorchard.com** for an up-to-date schedule. If you miss the festival, drop by Evan's Orchard in the summer for you-pick berries and in the fall for pumpkins, apples, and sweet treats.

Winchester's Driftwood Inn is credited for inventing beer cheese, a unique cheese spread combining sharp cheddar cheese and beer and traditionally served with carrots, celery, pretzels, and crackers.

The World Chicken Festival is home to the world's largest stainless steel skillet. It is ten feet six inches in diameter and eight inches deep, has an eight-foot handle, and weighs seven hundred pounds when empty. It requires three hundred gallons of cooking oil to fill and can cook six hundred quarters of chicken at one time.

Pronounced "ged-da" or "get-uh," this northern Kentucky tradition is a sausage with steel-cut oats and a collection of spices. German settlers brought it to the region in the eighteenth century.

The Beer Cheese Festival is held in downtown Winchester in June each year.

The International Bar-B-Q Festival in Owensboro began in the late 1970s and celebrates barbecue and burgoo. The festival's highlight is a fierce cooking competition in which teams from around the country compete for the best mutton, pork, chicken, and burgoo.

Each summer, thousands travel to Owensboro for the International Bar-B-Q Festival. On Saturday, cooking teams compete for top prizes, and visitors can purchase the winning meats.

Country ham is dry cured, meaning the ham is rubbed with salt and seasonings, smoked, and then aged anywhere from four months to three years.

The Trigg County Country Ham Festival is held each October in western Kentucky. You also have the opportunity to join the hog-calling contest.

Frying chicken is no easy feat, particularly when you have a colonel to live up to. Colonel Harland Sanders opened a roadside restaurant in Corbin, Kentucky, where he first served his famous fried chicken; it would become the Kentucky Fried Chicken restaurant franchise.

Facing: This odd Louisville staple is a cucumber and cream cheese spread invented around the turn of the twentieth century by Jennie Carter Benedict. It has been featured in *Southern Living*, *Garden & Gun*, *Saveur Magazine*, the *New York Times*, the *Washington Post*, the Food Network, and NPR.

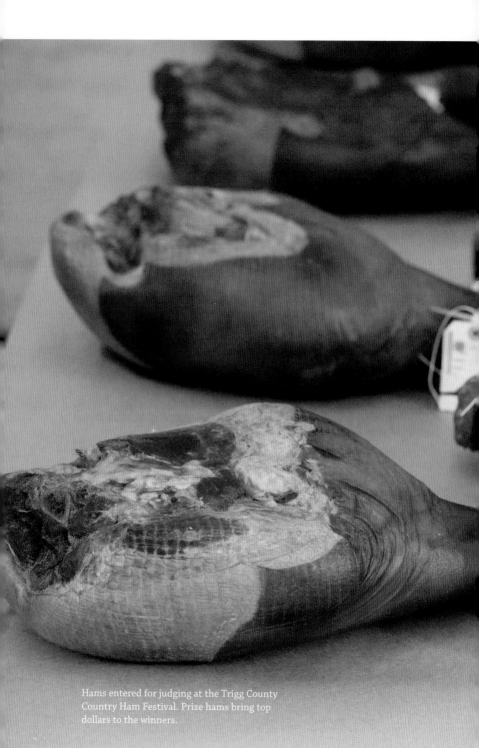

Hams entered for judging at the Trigg County Country Ham Festival. Prize hams bring top dollars to the winners.

TRIGG
COUNTY
4-H MEMBER
HAMS

The Trigg County Country Ham Festival is home to the World's Largest Country Ham and Biscuit, which weighs 2,000 pounds and measures 10.5 feet in diameter. It is cooked in a custom-built oven and removed by forklift during the festival.

A large chicken welcomes visitors to the annual World Chicken Festival in London, just ten miles north of where Kentucky Fried Chicken's Colonel Sanders opened his first chicken restaurant in Corbin.

All barbecue is popular in Kentucky, but in the western part of the state, mutton—or older sheep—became the most popular meat source due to an overabundance of aging sheep that had been retired from the fiber industry. Barbecuing the meat from the older animal made it tender enough to eat.

Produce sits on a judging table at the Trigg County Country Ham Festival. Community members enter items from their garden, baked goods, flowers, and country hams for judging at the annual event.

Sunflower seed (1 pint)

#3
A671

#1
A668

We call it race day pie because we can't call it Derby Pie. That name was literally drawn out of a hat by the Kern Family and trademarked. Only the Kerns can use the word *Derby* in the pie name, but most versions of May Day pie include chocolate chips, pecans, and bourbon.

The legendary Hot Brown was invented at Louisville's historic Brown Hotel by Chef Fred K. Schmidt. The stories say Schmidt didn't have many ingredients in the kitchen and was looking for a dish to excite late-night guests. The hotel still serves Chef Schmidt's recipe today.

Burgoo is a thick meat and vegetable stew that includes a variety of meats such as beef, pork, chicken, mutton, and rabbit and lots of veggies. Some versions are wilder and include whatever meat is convenient, from venison to squirrel and game birds. No two chefs make burgoo the same way.

Part Two
MAIN COURSES

3 | Burgoo

Burgoo is to Kentucky what Brunswick stew is to Virginia (or to Georgia, depending on who you ask). It is the Bluegrass State's version of Louisiana's famous gumbo. It's as much a staple to Kentuckians as clam chowder is to New Englanders. And while this historic dish can be traced back to the early days of the state, few culinary historians can agree on who, what, when, where, and why burgoo came about. They can't even seem to settle on an origin for the stew's name.

Is it *bur*-goo or bur-*goo*? Does the word come from bulgur porridge, which was a staple of sailors back in the 1700s? Is it a mash-up of barbecue and ragout, two filling—and frugal—dishes popular in the early days of Kentucky? Did the name come from French chef Gustave Jaubert, who worked for Confederate general John Hunt Morgan in the 1860s and is said to be the first person to make "bird stew," which with a French accent, could've been misheard as burgoo?

The not knowing is almost as fun as the quirky recipes for this culinary masterpiece.

Here is what we do know: burgoo is a thick meat and vegetable medley stew that generally includes a variety of meats, including beef, pork, chicken, mutton, and rabbit (or some combination of all of these—improvisation is key), and tomatoes, corn, potatoes, onions, lima beans, and okra. Some versions are

Copycat Keeneland Burgoo

1 cup diced celery

1 cup diced carrot

1 cup diced onion

3 pounds stew meat

12-ounce can tomato puree

2 pounds fresh okra, sliced

1 tablespoon beef base

1 teaspoon Worcestershire sauce

1 cup sherry wine

3 pounds diced potatoes

1 teaspoon ground thyme

1 teaspoon dry sage

1 teaspoon garlic powder

1 teaspoon dry oregano

Water (as needed)

Cornstarch (if desired)

Brown stew meat with herbs. Add remaining ingredients and cover with water. Bring to a boil, and reduce to simmer for a minimum of three hours, stirring occasionally. Before serving, combine water and cornstarch and add the mixture slowly, stirring until the burgoo reaches the desired thickness.

a little bit wilder and include whatever meat is convenient, from venison to squirrel to game birds; some burgoos contain barbecue. And no two chefs make burgoo the same way.

These fiercely guarded recipes are rooted in the history of Kentucky. Families still sit around the campfire, cooking enormous pots of stew so thick the spoon stands up in it and adding the ingredients that they happened to have—and everyone knows the best burgoos are stirred nonstop. A Kentucky tradition, whether started in the foothills of the Appalachian Mountains or by a French chef, burgoo remains a staple at family and church functions, political rallies, and racetracks across the Commonwealth (even the 1932 Kentucky Derby winner was named Burgoo King).

If you haven't tasted burgoo made by Chef Ed Boutilier at Keeneland Race Track in Lexington, you're missing out. Here is his famous recipe:

★ A ROAD TRIP TO THE ANDERSON COUNTY BURGOO FESTIVAL ★

The French chef Gustave Jaubert is often credited with being the Father of Burgoo. He was hired by Buffalo Trace Distillery in Frankfort shortly after the Civil War to cook for its employees and to cater small events (where he happened to serve John Hunt Morgan). He needed recipes that would serve a lot of people, and the stories go that he started making huge pots of "bird stew" from whatever ingredients were available to him. Louisville's *Courier-Journal* newspaper and the *New York Times* even published articles about Jaubert and mention him serving burgoo and barbecue.

Today, just down the road from Frankfort, visitors can help celebrate the storied history of Kentucky burgoo at the annual Anderson County Burgoo Festival in Lawrenceburg. The festival began in 1994 and celebrates the local roots of the hearty stew by inviting chefs to prepare their versions of burgoo. Each year,

Stoney Top Burgoo cooks up a batch of soup for visitors of the Anderson County Burgoo Festival in Lawrenceburg.

a winner is crowned, but let's be honest—all the sampling is the best part.

In addition to good eats, festival-goers can enjoy live music, a 5K run/walk, pageants, a Civil War reenactment, and more.

★ IF YOU GO

The festival takes place at the end of September each year in downtown Lawrenceburg, about fourteen miles south of Frankfort. Festivities begin on Friday and wrap up on Sunday. Visit **www.kentuckyburgoo.com** for up-to-date information.

★ A ROAD TRIP TO THE MOUNTAIN MUSHROOM FESTIVAL IN IRVINE ★

Have you ever had a Kentuckian ask you if you had any morels? They aren't after your behavioral standards or beliefs—we're mighty forgiving in that regard—they are asking if you've ever experienced the deliciousness that is the morel mushroom.

These mushrooms—often called America's mushrooms because they grow prominently across the country—come up in the spring and have inspired a culture of mountain mushroom hunters who chase after these natural delicacies. If you look for morels at your local grocery store, you could find yourself paying up to twenty dollars per pound. They aren't cheap! If you look for them in the woods of Kentucky, you have a long day of hunting for these camouflaged treasures ahead of you. It is a favorite pastime of Kentuckians, especially those who grew up in the mountainous region in the eastern part of the state.

The Mountain Mushroom Festival in Irvine celebrates the culture of Appalachia, including morel mushrooms, Kentucky agate (the state rock), and the region's arts and crafts, as well as the land that makes it unique, such as the Daniel Boone National Forest, the Kentucky River, and the Appalachian Mountains. The festival helps share the cultural heritage and traditions of the community while supporting local groups of mushroom hunters, agate collectors, craftspeople, artisans, and civic organizations. Visitors can enjoy mushroom hunts, agate and fossil expeditions, a mushroom market and cook-off, live entertainment, and more.

★ IF YOU GO

The Mountain Mushroom Festival is held in April each year in Irvine in Estill County, located about twenty miles east of Richmond. Admission is free. Visit **www.mountainmush roomfestival.org** for up-to-date information.

Facing: The Hot Brown, invented by chef Fred K. Schmidt at Louisville's Brown Hotel, is a stack of toasted bread, turkey, bacon, tomatoes, and cheese sauce.

FAMOUS KENTUCKY FLAVORS

4 | The Kentucky Hot Brown

We all know the feeling: we open the cabinets, peer into the empty refrigerator, and brush ice crystals from the freezer-burned frozen packages, but no matter how hard we look, there is absolutely nothing to eat. Sigh. When it happens to us, we can order takeout or grab our coats and run to our local grocery store. But when it happens at a hotel with a room full of hungry, waiting patrons, what's a chef to do?

That was exactly the big problem that led Chef Fred K. Schmidt to invent the Brown Hotel's famous Hot Brown. You see, in the 1920s, the Brown Hotel in downtown Louisville drew more than twelve hundred guests each evening for its dinner

The historic Brown Hotel located in downtown Louisville hosted dinner dances in the 1920s. Chef Fred K. Schmidt cooked the first Hot Brown for twelve hundred guests at one of these events.

dance. After a night of dancing, the guests had worked up quite the appetite, and they would make their way to the restaurant for a bite to eat.

One version of the story says that on a particularly busy night, Chef Schmidt was out of absolutely everything in his kitchen and was looking for savory ingredients to feed—and fill up—a room full of hungry and tired dancers. He pulled out all of the meats that he had—none of them enough to feed everyone—and started stacking a combination of bread, turkey, bacon, and cheese sauce together and placing it under the broiler to give it a little color.

Another version says Chef Schmidt was simply tired of the traditional ham and eggs and was looking for something more glamorous to serve his guests. No matter the story, he created a unique open-faced turkey sandwich with bacon and a delicate Mornay sauce that is a Kentucky tradition and favorite today.

The Brown Hotel still serves its famous Hot Brown (using Chef Schmidt's original recipe, no less), and this Louisville tradition has gained worldwide appeal through international media and some of the finest cookbooks. The hotel's perfected recipe

FAMOUS KENTUCKY FLAVORS

calls for heavy cream, pecorino Romano cheese, sliced roasted turkey breast, Texas toast, crispy bacon slices, Roma tomatoes, paprika, and parsley.

The Legendary Brown Hotel Hot Brown

(makes two Hot Browns)

1½ tablespoons salted butter

1½ tablespoons all-purpose flour

1½ cups heavy cream

¼ pecorino Romano cheese, plus extra for garnish

Pinch of ground nutmeg

Salt and pepper

14 ounces sliced roasted turkey breast, slice thick

4 slices Texas toast (crusts trimmed)

4 slices bacon

1 Roma tomato, sliced lengthwise

Paprika

Parsley

In a two-quart saucepan, melt butter and slowly whisk in flour until combined to form a thick paste or roux. Continue to cook the roux for two minutes over medium-low heat, stirring frequently. Whisk heavy cream into the roux and cook over medium heat until the cream begins to simmer, about two to three minutes. Remove sauce from heat and slowly whisk in pecorino Romano cheese until the Mornay sauce is smooth. Add nutmeg, salt, and pepper to taste.

For each Hot Brown, place one slice of toast in an oven-safe dish and cover with seven ounces of turkey. Cut the remaining pieces of toast in half diagonally and lean two toast points against the base of the sandwich. Then take two slices of Roma tomato and stack on top of the turkey. Pour half of the sauce over each dish, completely covering it. Sprinkle with additional cheese. Place entire dish under a broiler until cheese begins to brown and bubble. Remove and cross two pieces of crispy bacon on top. Sprinkle with paprika, parsley, and a bit more cheese, and serve immediately.

★ A ROAD TRIP TO THE HOT BROWN HOP IN LOUISVILLE ★

Visitors to Kentucky may try their hardest to survive on bourbon alone, but we recommend sampling some of our culinary treasures while you're here. Perhaps none of them are as iconically Kentucky as the Hot Brown, invented at Louisville's historic Brown Hotel in 1926. Today, the Hot Brown tradition is continued in many Louisville area restaurants.

While the traditional recipe is an open-faced hot sandwich that smothers turkey with Mornay sauce and tops it with bacon, chefs across Kentucky's largest city have tricks and twists to make it their own. Some variations add more ingredients, such as ham, crab meat, avocado, and mushrooms, and others modify the sandwich idea to create hot brown soups, pastas, and seafoods.

★ IF YOU GO ▶

The Louisville Convention and Visitors Bureau compiled a list of forty establishments that offer a Hot Brown on the menu. Follow this Hot Brown Hop to easily find the best places to indulge in the city's famed dish. Some favorites include Amici Cafe, Come Back Inn, Derby Cafe, the Highlands Tap Room Grill, the Troll Pub Under the Bridge, and Winston's Restaurant. For a complete list of restaurants on the Hot Brown Hop, visit **www.gotolouisville .com/culinary/things-to-do/hot-brown-hop**.

★ WHAT IN THE WORLD IS BENEDICTINE? ★

Ask a non-Kentuckian if they've ever had benedictine and they're probably going to make a funny, confused face at you and ask,

Facing: Benedictine is a spread made with cucumbers and cream cheese. It was invented by Jennie Carter Benedict in Louisville around the turn of the twentieth century.

"What's that?" That is, unless you're asking celebrity chefs Paula Deen or Damaris Phillips or anyone who has read articles about this spread in *Southern Living, Garden & Gun, Saveur Magazine,* the *New York Times,* the *Washington Post,* the Food Network, and NPR. In fact, benedictine may be the most famous unknown food out there. Or at least in Kentucky.

Benedictine is a spread made with cucumbers and cream cheese that was invented around the turn of the twentieth century by Jennie Carter Benedict, a caterer and cookbook author in Louisville. It was intended to be used for making cucumber sandwiches, but it can also come in dip form or can be combined with meat on a sandwich. For you tailgaters, benedictine is a favorite of Kentuckians to snack on before football games or during the spring and fall meets at Keeneland racetrack, where tailgating is a necessary pastime. You can buy the spread at nearly every grocery store or sandwich shop in the state, most popularly in central Kentucky between Lexington and Louisville.

While her restaurants have closed, you can still find Benedict's cookbooks today. Perhaps the most well-known is *The Blue Ribbon Cook Book,* which first published in 1902 and has been reprinted numerous times. While early editions of this book do not contain a benedictine recipe, the most recent edition does.

Benedictine

8 ounces cream cheese, softened

3 tablespoons cucumber juice

1 tablespoon onion juice

Salt to taste

Cayenne pepper to taste

2 drops green food coloring

Thoroughly blend all ingredients with a fork. You may substitute cucumber and onion juices with grated or chopped cucumbers and onions.

5 | Kentucky Fried Chicken

Have you ever tried frying chicken? It seems simple enough: a little buttermilk bath followed by a dip in some flour, and into the frying pan it goes. Go ahead and wipe off those hands and check this one off the list, right? If only.

Have you ever tried searching online, "how to fry chicken"? If you attempt the endeavor, thousands and thousands of results will flood in and for good reason—frying good chicken isn't just a science. It is an art.

Above: Fried chicken is widely popular in Kentucky largely due to the establishment of the Kentucky Fried Chicken restaurant franchise by Colonel Harland Sanders.

In the South, learning to fry chicken is a staple of growing up, much like learning to drive a car or learning how to do laundry without shrinking your favorite sweater. And it is no easy feat. Our grandmothers or great-aunts or uncles or parents usually teach us, and we never get it right on the first try. And in Kentucky, there is even more pressure to succeed with that buttermilk and that (preferably cast-iron) frying pan. Not only do we have to impress our culinary grandmothers, we also have to make rank with the colonel.

Colonel Harland Sanders is best known for founding the fast-food chain Kentucky Fried Chicken (perhaps more popularly known as KFC), which has restaurants across the globe. While he was technically born in Henryville, Indiana, in 1890, Kentuckians claim the colonel and his fried chicken because it was here that he invented his famous recipe and built his delicious empire.

Sanders got his start in the kitchen at a young age. His father died when he was just five years old, and Sanders became responsible for feeding and taking care of his younger brother and sister while his mother worked. He dropped out of school just two weeks into his seventh-grade school year, but he was a hard worker. The man was a farmer, streetcar conductor, railroad fireman, and insurance salesman, and by the time he was forty, Sanders was running a service station in Kentucky where he fed hungry travelers. His food was so popular that he moved his operation to a restaurant across the street and began perfecting his fried chicken recipe.

Happy with his now-famous eleven-herbs-and-spices formula, Sanders closed the restaurant in 1952 to focus on franchising his chicken business. Remember the Kaelin family, whom we told you about back in the introduction to this book? Well, Carl Kaelin may have been a culinary and business genius when it came to slapping a slice of cheese on a hamburger, but he evidently lacked some intuition. Hey, no one is perfect.

Facing: Colonel Harland Sanders is the culinary mastermind and businessman behind the Kentucky Fried Chicken restaurant franchise. He died in 1980 at the age of ninety and is buried at Cave Hill Cemetery in Louisville.

In the 1950s, Kaelin's Restaurant was a popular hangout, and Harland Sanders was a good friend of Carl Kaelin's. In the mid-1950s, Kaelin began serving Sanders's pressure-fried, specially seasoned chicken, and Sanders offered his friend a chicken franchise. According to local papers, Carl turned him down. He did, however, agree to sell Sanders's Original Recipe chicken, and volume at his restaurant on Newburg Road and Speed Avenue in Louisville increased so much that a new kitchen had to be built. Or so the story goes.

Sanders's chicken was so popular that Kentucky governor Ruby Laffoon named Sanders a Kentucky Colonel, the highest title of honor bestowed by the governor of Kentucky. This recognition of Sanders's noteworthy accomplishments and outstanding service to his community, state, and nation became almost as popular as his famous (and secret) fried chicken recipe. Harland Sanders became Colonel Sanders, which he is most notably called today.

The colonel devoted himself to franchising his chicken business, and in 1964, with more than six hundred franchised outlets, he sold his interest in his company for $2 million. Today, KFC Corporation remains based in Louisville. More than 185 million people see a KFC commercial at least once a week, and the system serves more than 12 million customers each day at its seventeen thousand restaurants in more than 115 countries and territories around the world.

The colonel died in 1980 at ninety years old, but his fried chicken legacy lives on through his KFC franchises and in the hearts of proud Kentuckians. He was a hard worker with high standards. One story Kentuckians like to tell is about an upset Colonel Sanders not understanding why KFC franchises were selling gravy that wasn't from his recipe. The corporate folks had to politely tell the colonel that most people couldn't keep up with his culinary standards and the gravy was simply too hard to make. We like that story because it speaks to the heart of Kentuckians in the kitchen. It may not be simple, but we'll still try our darndest to make it good.

While KFC holds Colonel Sanders's eleven herbs and spices close to the vest, we will share this similar fried chicken recipe with you and wish you the best of luck at your frying pan!

Kentucky Fried Chicken

1 whole chicken
(2 breasts, 2 thighs,
2 drumsticks, 2 wings)

2 quarts vegetable oil, for
frying

SPICE MIX:

1 tablespoon paprika

2 teaspoons onion salt

1 teaspoon chili powder

1 teaspoon black pepper

½ teaspoon celery salt

½ teaspoon dried sage

½ teaspoon garlic
powder

1 egg white

1½ cups all-purpose flour

1 tablespoon brown
sugar

1 tablespoon kosher salt

½ teaspoon ground
allspice

½ teaspoon dried
oregano

½ teaspoon dried basil

½ teaspoon dried
marjoram

Preheat fryer, cast-iron, or deep, thick-bottomed pan with oil to 350°. Thoroughly mix together all the spice mix ingredients. Combine spice mix with flour, brown sugar, and salt. Dip chicken pieces in egg white to lightly coat them, and then transfer to flour mixture. Turn a few times and make sure the flour mix is really stuck to the chicken. Repeat with all the chicken pieces. Let chicken pieces rest for five minutes so crust has a chance to dry a bit. Fry chicken in batches. Breasts and wings should take twelve to fourteen minutes, and legs and thighs will need a few more minutes. Chicken pieces are done when a meat thermometer inserted into the thickest part reads 165°F. Let chicken drain on a few paper towels when it comes out of the fryer. Serve hot.

★ A ROAD TRIP TO THE HARLAND SANDERS CAFE AND MUSEUM AND THE WORLD CHICKEN FESTIVAL ★

Kentuckians honor our colonel and his famous Kentucky Fried Chicken in the place where it all began. In the 1940s, Colonel Harland Sanders began serving fried chicken from his roadside restaurant on US Highway 25, between London and Corbin, Kentucky. The colonel later franchised his chicken restaurants, which became Kentucky Fried Chicken, but visitors can still stop by Harland Sanders Cafe and Museum for a taste of the famous chicken and to see memorabilia from the early days of the Kentucky Fried Chicken brand. If you like KFC, this is a must-see.

Above: London honors Colonel Harland Sanders and what they call the birthplace of chicken with the World Chicken Festival each September. Enjoy arts and crafts and a chicken dinner.

FAMOUS KENTUCKY FLAVORS

Sanders Cafe in Corbin is near the original restaurant on US Highway 25 where Colonel Harland Sanders first served his now famous fried chicken. Today, it is filled with memorabilia from the early days of Kentucky Fried Chicken.

We swear they cook up the best fried chicken of any KFC we've been to.

If you visit the museum at the end of September, drive less than ten miles north for the World Chicken Festival in London, Kentucky. This festival began in 1989 as a celebration of the life of Colonel Sanders and the chicken legacy he left behind. For you chicken aficionados, did you know that Lee's Famous Recipe Chicken also began in Kentucky? In Laurel County, in fact, home to London and next-door neighbor to Corbin, where Sanders got his start. Lee Cummings, cofounder of Lee's Famous Recipe, was Harland Sanders's nephew.

Today, events span an entire weekend in the fall and include entertainment, arts and crafts, carnival rides, a parade, and the always-popular clucking contest. Trust us—go for the clucking.

The festival is also home to the world's largest stainless steel skillet, which is operated by volunteers and has served more than 120,000 fried chicken dinners since its inauguration in 1992. The skillet is ten feet six inches in diameter and eight inches deep, has an eight-foot handle, and weighs seven hundred pounds when empty. It requires three hundred gallons of cooking oil to fill and can cook six hundred quarters of chicken at one time. At each festival, volunteers cook about seven thousand pieces of chicken, requiring 375 pounds of flour, 75 pounds of salt, 30 pounds of pepper, and 30 pounds of paprika. We can account for the consumption of at least four of those chicken quarters.

★ IF YOU GO ▶

The Harland Sanders Cafe and Museum is open year-round and is located at 688 US Highway 25 West in Corbin. The cafe doesn't currently have an actively updated website, but you can call (606) 528–2163 for information. The World Chicken Festival is held at the end of September each year in downtown London. Visit **www.worldchickenfestival.com** for updated information. Make sure to check the pavilion hours to see when they are serving chicken. You'll want to be there to see the world's largest skillet in action and to claim your generous fried chicken dinner. Trust us—you don't want to miss that deliciousness.

★ A ROAD TRIP TO THE GREEN RIVER CATFISH FESTIVAL ★

Since we're already elbow deep in the frying pan, let us recommend our second-favorite Kentucky fried delicacy: catfish. Each Fourth of July weekend, Morgantown, Kentucky, hosts the Green River Catfish Festival. This four-day festival includes fireworks, pageants, a dog show, a catfish cook-off (our personal favorite part), a car show, arts and crafts, square dancing, and carnival rides.

And because the only thing better than eating catfish is catching catfish (and then eating it), the festival is also the home of the Big Catfish Fishing Tournament. Each year, anglers fish for tagged catfish in the Green River for cash prizes. Come for the fishing and eating; stay for the fireworks.

★ IF YOU GO

Morgantown is located off of the William H. Natcher Parkway, about twenty-five miles northwest of Bowling Green. The festival is held at the Charles Black City Park. The event does not have a website, but follow **@greenrivercatfishfestival** on Facebook for annual updates on dates, exhibits, and cost of admission.

6 | Kentucky Barbecued Mutton

Emblazoned across a banner hanging from a tent at the International Barbecue Festival in Owensboro is the phrase "Mary Had a Little Lamb. Won't You Have Some, Too?" Now stop picturing the adorable, fluffy stuffed animals you find in stores at Easter and trust us on this one: you haven't experienced good barbecue until you've tried barbecued mutton.

As is often true with a story about the beginnings of barbecue, mutton's rise to popularity in Kentucky started with an

Above: Barbecue is a staple of Kentucky, and in the western part of the state, you are most likely to find mutton, or older sheep, as the meat of choice.

abundant supply of a particular type of meat for which normal cooking methods didn't work. Mutton is just what the nursery rhyme–inspired banner suggests: sheep. In particular, mutton is old sheep—usually over two years old and sometimes as old as four years. The early 1800s found western Kentucky with an abundance of old sheep. The Scotch and Irish immigrants who settled in this part of the state farmed sheep for their textiles, and as a result, wool production thrived during that time. The settlers soon realized that the wool-producing period of a sheep's life is considerably shorter than its lifespan. However, the older the animal gets, the less tender its meat is, so these farmers were faced with a problem. As it so often is, barbecue was the answer.

Barbecue is a way of cooking meat slowly at low temperatures with seasonings either through rubs or sauces. This method helps break down the fibers in tough meat and makes it tender and not just edible but tasty. In western Kentucky, after the sheep's wool-producing years passed, they were cooked over hot embers with lots of salt water, vinegar, and peppers. Cooking the meat over a low flame and saucing it constantly created a new style of barbecue.

Today, wool production isn't as abundant in Kentucky, but sheep farmers still raise older animals particularly for purchase by some of the state's most notable barbecue restaurants, such as Moonlite Bar-B-Q Inn and Old Hickory Bar-B-Q in Owensboro.

So you've gotten past your initial aversion to eating Mary's little lamb, and now you want to know what it tastes like, right? Rich and, despite sauces and seasonings, probably gamier than the pork barbecue that you're used to eating. For those of you who have tasted goat, mutton tastes a lot like that. Many people eat it as brisket, but we recommend the pulled variety with a vinegar and pepper barbecue sauce to add some tang—and heat! Pair with collard greens and enjoy!

Kentuckians have spent generations perfecting this particular barbecue, but it is most often found on restaurant menus in the western part of our state. Head west to Christian, Hopkins, and Trigg counties to start, and then go north into Henderson

The International Bar-B-Q Festival in Owensboro each summer is just one of more than three festivals celebrating delicious smoked meat in the Bluegrass State.

and Daviess counties. Owensboro is mutton central, and in addition to Moonlite and Old Hickory, we recommend Ole South Barbeque and Fritz's Barbeque Shack. If you're visiting the area in May, you can find all of our favorites and some hidden local talents in one place: the International Bar-B-Q Festival. It's one of our absolute favorite Kentucky events.

For those interested in trying mutton on your home barbecue pit, we won't offer you smoking advice (as every grill/pit master holds his or her secrets close to the vest), but we will suggest a great barbecue sauce for your meat.

A Good Mutton Barbecue Sauce

¼ cup Worcestershire sauce

1½ teaspoons brown sugar

¼ cup cider vinegar

2 teaspoons fresh lemon juice

1 teaspoon freshly ground black pepper

½ teaspoon coarse salt (kosher or sea)

½ teaspoon onion salt

½ teaspoon garlic powder

¼ teaspoon ground allspice

Blend together and apply to taste.

★ A ROAD TRIP TO KENTUCKY'S BARBECUE FESTIVALS ★

It speaks to Kentucky's affinity for good barbecue that the state hosts not one or two but *more than three* barbecue festivals each year. And none of them should be overlooked. Arguably—and yes, we're certain there is someone out there who would be happy to argue this with us—the largest is the International Bar-B-Q Festival, which takes place in Owensboro each May.

In the late 1970s, Catholic parishes in Daviess County were preparing eighty thousand pounds of mutton, eight thousand chickens, and thirty-one hundred pounds of pork each summer. Owensboro's barbecue restaurants were selling a combined forty thousand pounds of barbecue a week and one hundred gallons of burgoo (remember burgoo from chapter 2?) a day. That seemed reason enough for a celebration. In December 1978, the Owensboro-Daviess County Chamber of Commerce announced plans to create an international festival to celebrate barbecue and burgoo.

Today, the festival is attended by thousands, and its highlight is a fierce competition as cooking teams from around the country compete for prizes for the best mutton, pork, chicken, and burgoo, while raising money for local charities. Events are held in downtown Owensboro from Fourth Street to the beautiful riverfront parks along the Ohio River. Festivities include arts and crafts, carnival rides, entertainment, kids' activities, and of course, amazing food.

About 130 miles west along the Ohio River, you'll find another great Kentucky barbecue festival in Paducah. After you've had your summer barbecue in Owensboro, head to Paducah for Barbecue on the River in September. This barbecue festival began in 1994 to raise money for local charities, bring visitors to the streets of historic downtown Paducah, and celebrate great western Kentucky barbecue. This festival attracts cooking teams from across the country as well and more than eighty thousand pounds of chicken and pork are grilled, smoked, cooked, and (of course) eaten raising nearly $400,000 for local charities. Enjoy music, arts and crafts, and great food, and take time to enjoy everything Paducah has to offer.

Ready to head east? Well, we can't let our friends in the west have all the fun, now can we? In central Kentucky, barbecue lovers flock to Danville in early September for the Kentucky State BBQ Festival. This event features all our favorite things: good barbecue, good bourbon, and good entertainment. Danville invites celebrity pit masters to come cook for Kentuckians and has events for kids, arts and crafts vendors, and bourbon on hand. Originally held in downtown Danville, the festival moved to the grounds of the Wilderness Trail Distillery to allow room for expansion. More room for more barbecue? We'll raise our bourbon glasses to that.

★ IF YOU GO ►

If you're heading to Owensboro for the International Bar-B-Q Festival, make sure you're there on Saturday to sample what the cooking teams are smoking and to buy your favorites after winners are declared. The lines are long, but it's totally worth the wait. There's nothing quite like barbecue fresh off the pit! Visit **www.bbqfest.com** for up-to-date schedules and information.

While you're in Paducah for Barbecue on the River, take some time to enjoy downtown. It is one of our favorite My Old Kentucky Road Trip destinations. Enjoy great shops and museums, including the Paducah Railroad Museum and the National Quilt Museum, and if you're not too full from the great barbecue, stop at a local restaurant. For more information and a full festival itinerary, visit **www.bbqontheriver.org**.

If you're headed to Danville for the Kentucky State BBQ Festival, make sure to take a trip to Danville's historic Constitution Square. The original site of the festival, this park and open-air museum is still worth a stop while you're in the area. Also make time for a trip to some of the region's best bourbon distilleries. Four Roses Bourbon sponsors the barbecue festival, so start there. Visit **www.kybbqfestival.com** for updated information.

★ WHAT IN THE WORLD IS A LAMB FRY? ★

Now that we've desensitized you to eating lamb, let's discuss your willingness to try lamb fries. The word *fries* in this delicacy is a bit misleading. Lamb fries are, quite simply, sheep testicles that are sliced and fried and served with gravy. Still with us? We promise—they are better than they sound.

Lamb fries are served in a variety of cuisines, including Italian, Chinese, Armenian, and Turkish. In Kentucky's central Bluegrass region, we batter and deep-fry them. So why is this a Kentucky food staple? Well, no one is quite sure. Many attribute it to the same reason that mutton became popular—simply an overabundance of sheep in the state. No matter the reason, we recommend you giving them a try. You should try everything once, right?

For those of you interested—and brave enough—you can find lamb fries on the menu at Hall's on the River in Winchester and at Columbia Steakhouse in Lexington. Enjoy!

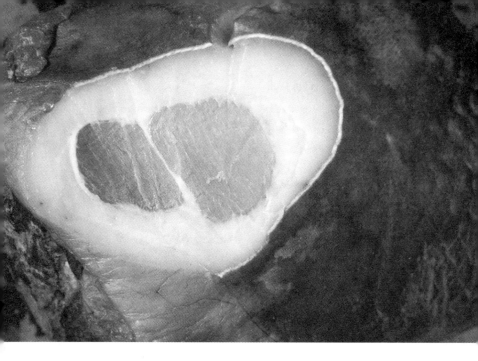

7 | Country Ham

No matter the lengths you go to, you would be hard-pressed to find anyone who would call country ham *artisanal*. But is this cured pork really all that different than prosciutto or capocollo? After all, it's a salt-cured ham that goes awfully well with crackers, if you don't mind us offering some food pairing advice.

Country ham is a Kentucky favorite and has been a part of life in the state since the first Europeans settled here and brought with them techniques for preserving meat through the winter. Country ham is dry cured, meaning the ham is rubbed with salt

Above: Country ham is dry cured, meaning the ham is rubbed with salt and seasonings, smoked, and then aged anywhere from four months to three years.

and seasonings, smoked, and then aged anywhere from four months to three years. The most popular methods involve placing the hams in salt boxes for about a month, dry rubbing them with pepper, and then hanging them from ceiling hooks where they are smoked at a low temperature using hickory wood for up to five weeks. Then the aging process—which often lasts right around a year but can stretch to several years—begins. The end product is intensely salty and chewy and usually served with biscuits.

In Kentucky, we may not have invented the country ham, but we sure know how to take it to the next level. Travel to the Trigg County Country Ham Festival in western Kentucky if you want to see the world's largest—*Guinness Book of Records* official—country ham and biscuit. And if you happen to be at the Kentucky State Fair, stop by the Kentucky Farm Bureau's annual Ham Breakfast to see a country ham that is more expensive than a Rolls Royce. No, we aren't joking.

It is a tradition that began in 1964 as a way to promote the pork industry in the state. Interested bidders could buy a ticket at the door and win a ham for a few hundred dollars. That was then. In 2014, the prized country ham went for a whopping $2 million, and new records have been set since. Today, the ham breakfast has grown to nearly 2,000 attendees and is a highlight of the ten-day fair.

So maybe country ham should be placed on that artisanal pork and cheese platter, huh?

Red Eye Gravy

Country ham slices (leave grease in skillet)

½ cup water or black coffee

Sauté country ham slices in a hot skillet. Remove from pan and add water or black coffee. Simmer about three minutes while stirring to collect drippings. Serve over ham slices with hot biscuits and grits.

Each October, Cadiz, Kentucky, celebrates country ham with the Trigg County Country Ham Festival, home of the World's Largest Country Ham and Biscuit.

The process of preparing, curing, cooking, storing, and even carving your country ham is a long and detailed one, so we won't try to teach you here. However, if you're looking for tips, let us point you toward Colonel Bill Newsom's Aged Kentucky Country Ham (**newsomscountryham.com**). They offer a lot of detail and great help through that process. And if you're looking to buy a ham already prepared, we recommend Broadbent's (**broadbenthams.com**). What we can offer you is a great pairing suggestion if you want your country ham on something other than a plain biscuit. We recommend country ham with red eye gravy.

★ A ROAD TRIP TO THE TRIGG COUNTY COUNTRY HAM FESTIVAL ★

Listen, we'll be the first to admit that we have an enthusiastic affinity for food festivals. We're always up for a weekend trip of arts and crafts, live music, and cooking and/or eating competitions of any kind. But if you add in a Guinness World Record–holding world's largest anything, consider our enthusiasm quadrupled.

Perhaps this is why we make an annual pilgrimage to the Trigg County Country Ham Festival in Cadiz each fall. We enjoy the vendors and the rides, the bluegrass music on the bales of straw, and the hog-calling contest (you absolutely have to enter if you visit), but the best part is the World's Largest Country Ham and Biscuit.

The enormous biscuit debuted in 1985 during the ninth annual Ham Festival. It weighed 4,000 pounds. A crowd of over fifteen thousand people were on hand to view the biscuit, and a parade was held in its honor, grand marshaled by University of Kentucky basketball coach Joe B. Hall. He's more revered in Kentucky than the queen is in England. Scout's honor. The recipe has since been halved, and each year a mere 2,000-pound biscuit, measuring 10.5 feet in diameter, is baked in a custom-built oven and removed by forklift during the festival. The recipe includes 150 pounds of flour, 2 pounds of salt, 6½ pounds of sugar, 39 pounds of shortening, 39 cups of water, 13 gallons of buttermilk. Add sixteen large baked country hams, and it is served to the hungry masses.

★ IF YOU GO

While the festival did away with its Sack the Pig contest years ago, there is fun for the entire family. The festival is held on Main Street in Cadiz in October each year. Check out **hamfestival .com** for event itineraries and more information. The World's Largest Country Ham and Biscuit is served on Saturday morning in the parking lot of the Bank of Cadiz.

★ A ROAD TRIP TO TATER DAY IN BENTON ★

On the first weekend in April each year, Benton in western Kentucky celebrates Tater Day. This event, which marks the community's unofficial start to spring, is one of the oldest festivals in the state and the oldest continuous trade day in the United States. It grew out of the county court day, first held in 1843, when farmers would take advantage of the opportunity to sell or trade their livestock, produce (including their potatoes, or as we say in Kentucky, "taters"), guns, and farm equipment in the town square.

Today, the community celebrates with carnival rides, arts and crafts vendors, a biggest potato contest, a potato-eating contest, food vendors, a parade, and more.

★ IF YOU GO

The annual Tater Day celebration is held along Main Street in Benton, located off the Purchase Parkway about twenty-five miles southeast of Paducah. The festival doesn't have a website, so check **explorekentuckylake.com** for updated information. It is usually held on the weekend before the first Monday in April.

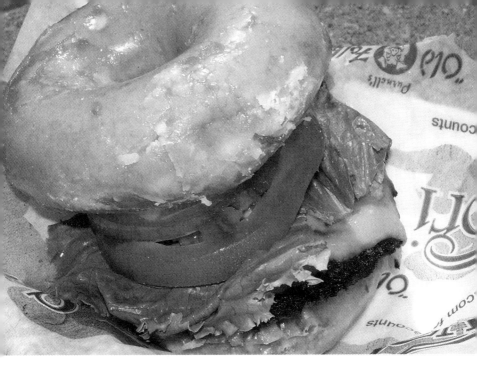

8 | Kentucky State Fair Food

Each August, Kentuckians flock to the state fairgrounds in Louisville for a week of games, carnival rides, livestock competitions, horse shows, great music, and some of the best food Kentucky has to offer—or if not the best, certainly the most unique.

The Kentucky State Fair is a mecca for foodies who are interested in tasting unique fair fares and state flavorites (see what we did there?). The usual fair staples, such as funnel cakes, corn dogs, smoked turkey legs, and nachos, are always available, but trust us—you're going to want to get out of your dietary comfort zone and discover new flavors you never expected could ever go together. Be brave!

Food booths at fairs appeared around 1900, mostly to sell local meats and baked goods. At the 1904 World's Fair in St. Louis, the introduction of waffle cones, cotton candy, hot dogs, and Dr. Pepper ushered in the modern era of novelty foods. The Texas State Fair debuted the foodsicle concept when they unveiled the corndog in 1942. Today, concessionaires dedicate themselves to one-upping each other with the oddest and most shocking food creations each year—most of them deep-fried and on a stick, to our utmost delight.

Kentucky does its part to contribute to the food culture shock of the state fair. One year, the Krispy Kreme burger sandwiched an all-beef patty, bacon, lettuce, tomato, and mayo between two glazed donuts. And if that wasn't enough of a shock, a few years later we met the Philly cheesesteak donut burger, which—you guessed it—placed a traditional Philly cheesesteak on a donut bun. The Kentucky State Fair has tried its hand at a popular Canadian favorite, poutine. But to put a Bluegrass spin on things, we topped our deep-fried potatoes with everything sweet or savory that you could dream up. Some were smothered in caramel, maple syrup, and marshmallows. Others were topped with pulled pork, cheese, and barbecue sauce. And because nothing is off limits for vendors at the Kentucky State Fair, visitors can also taste butt fries, which consist of smoked pork butt, cheddar cheese sauce, red onions, jalapeno peppers, and barbecue sauce on top of fries.

For those with a sweet tooth, skip the deep-fried Oreos and try the deep-fried Derby Pie. There's nothing more Kentucky than that.

The Kentucky State Fair is an annual celebration of agriculture, state culture, business, and community. Held at the Kentucky Exposition Center in Louisville, the fair runs for ten days and features entertainment for the whole family.

★ A ROAD TRIP TO THE KENTUCKY STATE FAIR ★

If the culinary escapades aren't enough to get you to the Kentucky State Fair, let us tempt you with more of its attractions. The state fair is one of our absolute favorite Kentucky events each year. It brings together citizens from across the Commonwealth and celebrates our state's culture of agriculture, business, and community. If you have never watched a sunset from the top of a fair Ferris wheel, we beg you to give it a try sometime soon. There is just nothing like it.

The fair stretches ten days at the end of August each year and is the perfect way to end a hot Kentucky summer. Enjoy livestock shows and awards, pageants, talent shows, petting zoos, carnival rides, community booths, arts and crafts competitions, and concerts, and have we mentioned the food? More than six hundred thousand people fill the 520 acres of indoor and outdoor exhibits over the ten days. Come be a part of it!

★ IF YOU GO ▶

The Kentucky State Fair is held at the Kentucky Exposition Center in Louisville. Exhibits are both indoors and outdoors, so prepare for weather—bring sunscreen, comfortable shoes, and an umbrella just in case—but know there is an indoor area to duck into when you get too hot or the rain comes down a little too hard. A full schedule of daily events and concerts, along with admission costs and driving and parking directions, is available at **kystatefair.org**.

★ WHAT IN THE WORLD IS A HEMP HOT DOG? ★

The state fair isn't necessarily known for its health foods (deep-fried pie and caramel-and-marshmallow-covered tater tots aren't exactly food pyramid approved), and it has sometimes been the

Kentucky Dawgs with hemp are all-beef hot dogs infused with hemp that debuted at the Kentucky State Fair in 2016. This Kentucky Proud product helps bring together the state's beef producers and its newly revitalized hemp industry.

complaint of fairgoers that the event brings in too much food from outside vendors and doesn't offer enough local meat. In a state with a thriving beef cattle industry, this just isn't acceptable. But in recent years, Kentucky beef is getting assistance from a most unlikely superhero.

Hemp is a crop that once had a big impact on the state of Kentucky. But that was decades ago. Since then, its close relation to marijuana has given the crop a bad rep (apparently our mothers were right when they told us that we would be judged by the company we keep). But Kentucky cattle farmers and the Kentucky Cattlemen's Association have partnered with the state's newly revitalized hemp industry to serve up a new state fair favorite: Kentucky Dawgs. These locally sourced and processed all-beef hot dogs are cooked with hemp oil and a sprinkling of crushed hemp hearts to add a roasted nut flavor to the quarter-pound bratwurst.

Don't worry—hemp oil and seeds are permitted ingredients for flavoring meat by the US Department of Agriculture, and no, hemp isn't harmful. Hemp contains no THC, the high-inducing compound in marijuana.

So why hemp? Well, why not? By infusing a beef hot dog with hemp, its creators achieved the shock value that is so often associated with strange state fair fare. It is certainly a unique creation. But more than that, these Kentucky Dawgs are one of the healthier options at the state fair and provide a product that could have potential impact on local beef and hemp farmers.

We can tell you from experience that these hemp hot dogs are definitely worth trying. For locals, Kentucky Dawgs are available at some central Kentucky Kroger grocery stores.

Part Three
DESSERTS

9 | Derby and Transparent Pies

All eyes turn to Kentucky during the first weekend in May for the infamous Kentucky Derby. Often referred to as the most famous two minutes in sports, the Kentucky Derby is attended by people from across the globe, and it gives us the opportunity to introduce the world to everything that Kentucky has to offer. Come for the Derby, and we Kentuckians are likely to recommend a mint julep first and a slice of Derby Pie second.

Because we don't want to anger our lawyers, let us take this moment to correct ourselves. We'll recommend a mint julep first

Above: Race day pie (sometimes called May Day pie) is a delicious combination of bourbon, chocolate chips, and pecans. It is a Kentucky staple with a storied history.

and a slice of May Day pie second. Or we could call it race day pie or chocolate-pecan-bourbon pie. We include this clarification because the Derby Pie® was invented more than fifty years ago as the specialty pastry of the Melrose Inn in Prospect, Kentucky, just outside of Louisville. George Kern, manager of the restaurant, developed the Derby Pie® recipe with the help of his parents, Walter and Leaudra. Many other culinary types have made

Race Day Pie

1 basic pie dough (we won't judge if you use the store-bought version)

6 large eggs

1 large egg yolk

1⅓ cups dark corn syrup

⅓ cup packed light brown sugar

4 tablespoons unsalted butter (½ stick), melted

2 tablespoons bourbon (your choice)

1 tablespoon vanilla extract

½ teaspoon kosher salt

2 cups whole pecans, toasted

4 ounces semisweet chocolate chips

Heat the oven to 350 degrees, and place your oven rack in the lower third. Line a 9½-inch deep dish pie plate with dough, and trim off excess. Bake until dough is slightly brown, approximately twenty to thirty minutes. Remove from the oven, and raise the oven temperature to 375 degrees. Whisk together eggs, egg yolk, corn syrup, brown sugar, butter, bourbon, vanilla, and salt in a medium bowl until smooth, about one minute. Add nuts and chocolate chips, and mix until evenly combined. Pour into crust, and bake until filling is set, slightly puffed, and dark brown, about thirty-five to forty minutes. Remove to a wire rack, and let cool completely before cutting. Serve cold or at room temperature.

Similar in consistency to chess pie, transparent pie was made famous by Magee's Bakery in Maysville in the 1930s and remained popular because it was inexpensive to make.

similar pies with similar names—May Day pie was a staple in our households growing up—but don't for a minute think you can go to a restaurant and ask for a Derby Pie®. The Kerns trademarked the term in 1968 and don't appreciate others using the name; they've sued to protect their trademark more than twenty-five times. The family closed the Melrose Inn in the 1960s but kept the pie business, and today they operate a commercial kitchen in Louisville, where they still bake and ship their famous (and patented) Derby Pie®.

So how did the pie get its famous trademarked and often-copied name? According to the Kern family, it was literally pulled out of a hat. No one could agree on a name for the baked treat, so they tossed some suggestions in a hat, and Derby Pie® came out.

The Kerns keep their recipe a secret to this day, but we'll tell you it involves walnuts, chocolate chips, and absolutely no bourbon. This is a point worth noting because most other May Day pie recipes result in a sort of embellished pecan pie with a sweet, sticky filling made with bourbon, chocolate chips, and pecans.

Maysville's Historic Transparent Pie

½ cup (1 stick) butter, melted

2 cups sugar

1 cup cream

4 eggs, beaten

2 tablespoons flour

1 teaspoon vanilla extract

1 unbaked 9-inch pie shell

Beat butter and sugar in a mixing bowl. Add cream and mix well. Beat in eggs. Stir in flour and vanilla. Pour into pie shell. Bake at 375 degrees for forty minutes or until golden brown.

Yum, right? We obviously can't share the Kern's Derby Pie® recipe, but here is a great race day pie variation that we would love to take a bite of (naturally, we included bourbon).

While we have the attention of your sweet tooth, let us recommend a second Kentucky favorite for pie lovers who aren't in the mood for chocolate (we don't get it, but we acknowledge the preference exists). For those of you who like chess pie, you will love Kentucky's transparent pie.

The pie first started appearing in Kentucky newspaper advertisements in the 1890s and is a close relative to Indiana's sugar pie, New England's chess pie, and Pennsylvania's shoofly pie. It was widely popularized in the state by Magee's Bakery, which started in Maysville in the 1930s and today has a location in Lexington. Transparent pie became popular across the state because it was simple and affordable for families to make (it didn't call for expensive pecans).

It's a pretty simple pie to make with just a few ingredients, including sugar, eggs, and milk. While it isn't truly transparent, the pie gets its name because its filling is colorless.

Do you need one more reason to give transparent pie a try? It is a favorite of Maysville native George Clooney. When the actor makes it back to Kentucky, he's been known to get a few transparent pies (and the tart version) to take back to Hollywood.

★ A ROAD TRIP TO THE PECAN FESTIVAL IN HICKMAN ★

With all those May Day pies, we need a few pecan farms to keep us in supply. Most Kentucky pecan growers are located in the western part of the state and in Hickman, the community celebrates the tree nut with a festival each September. Hickman is situated on the Mississippi River, across from Missouri. Home to the Kentucky Nut Corporation, the community knows a thing or two about pecans.

The Pecan Festival includes a community-wide yard sale, arts and crafts vendors, music in the park, bingo, a veterans' event, a barbecue cook-off, children's activities, and live entertainment.

★ IF YOU GO ▶

The event doesn't have an active website, so follow Hickman Recreation and Tourism on Facebook, **@hickmanrecreation tourism**, for updates and for more activities in the river town. From Western Kentucky Parkway, follow the Purchase Parkway south to Kentucky Highway 166 west, and take Kentucky Highway 125 north into Hickman. Bring your fishing poles! The event takes place at Jeff Green Memorial Park, a great place to catch the big one.

★ A ROAD TRIP TO THE BANANA FESTIVAL IN FULTON ★

Now, don't for one minute think there aren't festivals across the Commonwealth celebrating the healthier items on the food pyramid.

Travel southwest to Fulton, Kentucky, and you'll discover a unique town boasting an equally unique festival. Fulton is situated on the Kentucky-Tennessee state line, directly across the border from South Fulton, Tennessee. Each September, the twin cities host one of our favorite events: the Banana Festival. For those of you wondering if Kentucky weather is conducive to growing bananas, we'll go ahead and break the news to you: it really isn't. But Fulton and its sister city, South Fulton, have had a great impact on bananas in the United States.

When refrigerated railroad cars were invented in 1880, folks in North America could enjoy tropical fruits year-round. The United Fruit Company, now Chiquita, began shipping bananas from South America to New Orleans, where they were loaded into railcars and placed on top of 162-pound blocks of ice. Fulton had the only icehouse on the route north to Chicago.

The bananas were re-iced with blocks from the Fulton Ice Plant, which has since closed, and continued their journey north. For a time, Fulton was called the Banana Capital of the World, because 70 percent of the bananas consumed in the United States passed through Fulton. Now there's a reason for a festival if we've ever heard one.

Over the years, the Fulton Banana Festival has hosted congresspeople, governors, and Latin American guests from Ecuador, El Salvador, Guatemala, Honduras, Costa Rica, Peru, Colombia, Panama, Nicaragua, Mexico, Argentina, and Venezuela.

While you can enjoy the usual arts and crafts and food vendors, the highlight of the festival has always been its one-ton banana pudding (the world's largest, of course). After traveling in the parade, the pudding is distributed to visitors. It's about time, right?

★ IF YOU GO

The festival is held in September each year between Walnut and Main streets in downtown Fulton. Events take place across an entire week, stretching Saturday to Saturday. If you're going for the banana pudding (and we suggest that you do), you'll want to go on the concluding Saturday. Visit **thebananafestival.com** for annual dates, directions, and a full schedule of events.

Looking for more fruit festivals? Kentucky is proud to be home to the Casey County Apple Festival (**caseycounty applefestival.org**), which includes arts and crafts, food and flea market booths, and the world's largest apple pie (well, naturally) every September.

10 | Bourbon Balls

At this point, it should come to as no surprise that Kentuckians seem to like two things above all others: bourbon and food. So imagine our elation at the possibility of combining the two. Rebecca Ruth Candy appeals to our state pride and our taste buds with its world-famous bourbon balls.

We're absolutely certain that the candy company, based in Frankfort, makes other varieties of sweets. But it is perhaps most famous (and certainly most respected by Kentuckians) for inventing a unique and distinctively Kentucky candy in the bourbon ball. While you may be able to find the treat across the country today, Ruth Hanly originally got the idea for mixing up a sugary bourbon filling at Frankfort's sesquicentennial celebration in 1936 at the suggestion of dignitary Eleanor Hume Offutt. Ruth worked on the recipe for two years before perfecting the still-secret process.

Rebecca Ruth Candy was founded in Frankfort in 1919 by two substitute schoolteachers, Ruth Hanly and Rebecca Gooch. Each holiday season, they would make chocolates for friends and family, and after years of praise, they decided they were better candymakers than substitute teachers. Not many women went into business in the early twentieth century, but Rebecca and Ruth rented the barroom at the Frankfort Hotel (which was closed due to Prohibition) and began making chocolates on a twelve-foot marble table. The table became iconic for the candy company. It was originally a bar top in the Old Capitol Hotel dating back to around 1850, and Ruth purchased the marble slab in 1917 for ten dollars. Eventually, the table was named Edna's Table, after an employee who worked for Rebecca Ruth Candies for sixty-seven years before retiring at age ninety.

Today, the candy company is run by Ruth's son, John, and his son Charles. The candy factory is open to tours daily at its location just blocks from the Capitol building in Frankfort. Tour highlights include seeing Edna's Table and an antique candy furnace with hand-stirred copper kettles still in use today. The factory is located at 116 East Second Street in Frankfort. Learn more at **rebeccaruth.com**.

And while Rebecca Ruth claims to have invented the bourbon ball, Kentucky's iconic candy are available at other candy retailers and at the many bourbon distilleries across the state. Dedicate some time to sampling bourbon balls made from your favorite brands of Kentucky straight bourbon whiskey. We promise you won't regret it.

Bardstown hosts the Kentucky Bourbon Festival each year with live music, arts and crafts, and, most importantly, bourbon tastings.

★ A ROAD TRIP TO THE KENTUCKY BOURBON FESTIVAL IN BARDSTOWN ★

What's the one thing better than celebrating Kentucky bourbon? Try celebrating bourbon among tens of thousands of fellow Kentuckians and bourbon enthusiasts. This huge annual festival mixes black-tie events with golf outings, hot rod runs, and family fun. Oh, and there is a lot of bourbon to drink there, too.

Each year in September, Bardstown's thirteen thousand residents more than triple for a week. Rain or shine—we've been there for both, and we suggest boots in the rain—the Kentucky Bourbon Festival is a six-day event of smooth bourbon, delicious food, great entertainment, and a healthy dose of Kentucky hospitality. It's our absolute favorite.

★ IF YOU GO

Head to One Court Square in Bardstown around the middle of September each year, and prepare your palates. Each brand has a tent, and each tent has a taste. There are also events for kids and families, including arts and crafts, live music, food, shows, and plenty of Kentucky culture. The festival is free, but some events charge admission. Visit **kybourbonfestival.com** to learn more.

★ WHAT IN THE WORLD IS A BLUE MONDAY? ★

A Blue Monday is what our mothers might fondly call a throwback to the old-fashioned candy bars you may remember from childhood (read: from the 1950s and '60s). Invented by Kentucky candy maker Ruth Hunt (not be confused with Ruth Hanly, of Rebecca Ruth Candy fame—you have to keep up), Blue Mondays are a soft candy made of sugar, cream, and butter surrounded by semisweet chocolate. They remain the company's most popular treat today. Perhaps the coolest part about them is that Blue

The Blue Monday candy bar is a cream-and-sugar-filled chocolate bar invented by Ruth Hunt Candy Company in Mt. Sterling.

Mondays are made using a ninety-year-old recipe, and much of the production process is still done by hand.

According to the company, the Blue Monday was named by a traveling minister who once remarked, "Every Monday I have to have a little sweet to help me through my blue Monday." But trust us—you can enjoy a Blue Monday any day of the week.

Ruth Hunt Candy Company is located in Mt. Sterling, Kentucky, about thirty-six miles east of Lexington down Interstate 64. You can watch the production of Blue Mondays as well as the company's other candy most days of the week on a factory tour. Visit **ruthhuntcandy.com** to learn more.

Cameron M. Ludwick is a bookworm, trivia nerd, and former band geek who still relies on the survival skills she learned at Girl Scout camp to cope with nature. A Kentucky native, she now has bigger hair and lives in Austin, Texas.

Blair Thomas Hess is a born-and-bred Kentuckian who once won a sack-the-pig contest at the Trigg County Country Ham Festival. She resides in Frankfort, Kentucky, with her daughter and her picture-taking, bourbon-collecting husband.

Together, these longtime friends travel across the commonwealth of Kentucky, exploring its various wonders and uncovering its best-kept secrets.

Follow the adventure at **myoldkentuckyroadtrip.com** and on Twitter (**@MyOldKYRoadTrip**) and Instagram (**@myoldkentuckyroadtrip**).